THOUGHTS AND FEELINGS

Our Stepfamily

Julie Johnson

Aladdin / Watts

London • Sydney

Contents

Our Stepfamily

© Aladdin Books Ltd 2007

Designed and produced by
Aladdin Books Ltd
2/3 Fitzroy Mews
London W1T 6DF

First published in 2007
by Franklin Watts
338 Euston Road
London NW1 3BH

Franklin Watts Australia
Level 17/207 Kent Street
Sydney NSW 2000

Franklin Watts is a division of Hachette Children's Books.

ISBN 978 0 7496 7497 7

A catalogue record for
this book is available
from the British Library.

Illustrator: Christopher O'Neill

The author, Julie Johnson, is a health education consultant and trainer,
working with parents, teachers, carers and organisations such as Kidscape.

Dewey Classification:
306.874

Introduction

These children are friends. Each one of them is a member of a stepfamily. Families come in many different shapes and sizes. Stepfamilies are just one kind of family. The children in this book will share their thoughts and feelings about having a stepparent, stepbrothers and stepsisters.

A stepfamily has its ups and downs, just like any family.

I live with Mum. I visit Dad and my other stepfamily.

I see my dad and my stepfamily at weekends.

I live with my stepmum and Dad, but I still see my natural mum.

What Are Stepfamilies?

Grace's dad and mum split up a few years ago. Grace's dad has a new partner called Kate. Kate is Grace's stepmum. Leah is telling Grace that being a member of a stepfamily is just like being in any family except that a stepfamily is made from two families, or one family and another grown-up.

You may have a stepparent...

My stepfamily's almost big enough to be a football team!

In my stepfamily, there's me, my stepmum and my dad.

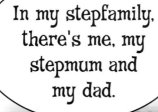

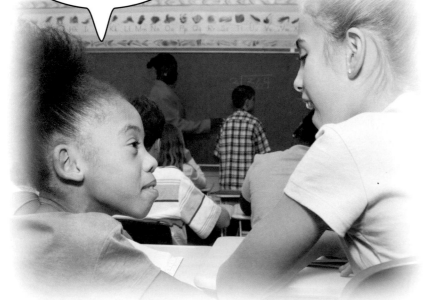

...and stepbrothers and -sisters.

▶ Two Mums

A stepfamily is the coming together of two adults, one or both of whom have children from a previous relationship. This means that you may have two mums – your natural mum and a stepmum. You can love them both in different ways.

◀▼ Little Or Large?

A stepfamily may be small or quite large if your stepparent already has his or her own children. If both your parents have new partners, you may even have two stepfamilies!

Leah, how do people come to be in a stepfamily?

"Stepfamilies can happen for lots of reasons. Dad died when I was a baby. Then Mum married Paul, my stepdad. My sister, Mum and I went to live with Paul and his children. Grace has a stepfamily because her parents split up and her dad remarried."

Stepparents

Alex is telling Charlie how much he enjoys his regular visits to see his mum, stepdad and stepbrothers. For most of the time, Alex lives with his natural dad and he gets on really well with his stepdad, too. But you may be more like Charlie. It took him a long time to accept and to like his stepmum.

Accepting new people can be hard.

9

Will I ever get used to being a parent?

▼ I Miss My Mum

You may blame your stepparent for your natural parents splitting up. It's quite natural to feel like this. But try to remember that blaming people or feeling cross won't change the situation.

▲ Help!

For some grown-ups, becoming a stepparent is their first go at being a parent. Your stepparent may be worried about how you will all get on and if you will like him or her. Try to remember that grown-ups can feel nervous, too!

▶ I'm Confused!

You may feel confused if you love your natural parent, but also get on well with your new stepparent. Your natural mum or dad will always be special to you, but it is not wrong to care about your new parent. You can love people in different ways.

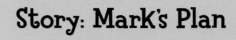

Stepparents

Story: Mark's Plan

1 Mark thinks that his mum will stop loving Colin, his stepdad, if he is unfriendly to him.

2 Mark tells his mum that he doesn't like Colin because he's not his natural dad.

3 Colin tries to make friends with Mark but nothing seems to work.

Why is Mark being so unfriendly?

Mark misses his natural dad and is determined not to like Colin. He feels that Colin is trying to take the place of his dad. But being unfriendly to Colin will not make his mum and his natural dad get back together. Colin doesn't want to take the place of Mark's dad. He just wants to be a good friend to Mark.

▶ Feeling Jealous

If you live with your stepfamily you may also want to spend time with the parent from whom you live apart. This is not always possible, but remember that it's OK to love your stepparent and your natural parent.

> I'll never like Paul because he's not my real dad.

> I do get on with my stepmum but it's so nice when I spend time with my mum.

◀ Feelings

If you find it very hard to accept or to like your stepparent, tell your other parent how you feel. Talking about your feelings doesn't make a problem go away, but it can help to make you feel better.

Charlie, how do you feel about having a mum and a stepmum?
"At first I didn't want to like Janice, my stepmum, because I missed my natural mum. But Mum explained that I can love them in different ways. I still see my mum at weekends and she'll always be my mum. We have a great time together, but I can have a good time with Janice, too."

Stepbrothers And -Sisters

Pattie and Jess both have stepbrothers and -sisters, as well as their own natural brothers and sisters. It can take time to get used to having a stepbrother or -sister. Remember that stepbrothers and -sisters can fall out and be best of friends, just like any brothers and sisters!

It's not always easy to join in.

They all look nice. I like my stepbrothers now, but when I first met them they just ignored me.

I found it hard at first, too, but we get on OK now. This photo is of us all on holiday.

▶ Quiet Time

You may sometimes want to spend some quiet time with your natural mum or dad, rather than always seeing him or her with your stepbrothers or -sisters. There is nothing wrong in wanting to do this.

Nobody listens to me anymore.

◀ What About Me?

Having new stepbrothers and -sisters can mean that you suddenly have to share your natural parent with lots of other people. This may make you feel fed up and a bit jealous, too.

▶ Feeling Left Out

If you feel left out or find it hard to get on with your stepbrothers or -sisters, tell your natural parent or stepparent how you feel. He or she may not be able to make the problem go away immediately, but it can help to tell someone how you feel.

I can understand you felt left out. I'm glad you told me.

Story: Living Together

1 Before Dan and his daughter, Rosie, moved in, Polly had her own room.

2 Polly felt really cross and fed up when Rosie moved into her room.

3 After a while, they got used to sharing a room. They even enjoyed it!

Why didn't Polly want to share her room with Rosie?

Polly didn't ask for a stepsister, but she got one, and she had to share her room with her! Sharing things with a stepbrother or -sister can be hard if, like Polly, you have not had to do so before. It's not easy accepting situations which you have not chosen, but sometimes they work out better than you think!

▶ A New Friend In The Family

Some stepbrothers and -sisters hit it off straight away. It may be that you have not liked being an only child and now have someone to spend time with. A stepbrother or -sister can become a good friend!

We don't want you to play with us.

◀ Help Make It Easy

If you are a member of a large family and a step-brother or -sister comes to visit or to stay with you, make an effort to include him or her in your games. You may not be best friends, but it helps to be friendly.

Jess, tell us how you get on with your stepbrothers and stepsisters.

"At first my sister and I didn't like them. But we all tried really hard and we get on most of the time now. It's nice having Emma, who is older than I am. It's fun playing football with the boys but they can be a pain at times, just like all brothers."

Getting Used To Change

When Gary and his dad moved in with Gary's stepmum, Gary had to move school. He had to get used to a different way of doing things with his dad and stepmum, and another way of doing things with his mum and stepdad! Becoming part of a stepfamily can mean lots of change.

You may have to move house.

I didn't want to move house or change schools, but I like it here now.

Yeah, it's a good laugh at school.

▶ Does It Feel Ok?

A new family may also mean moving house and going to a new school. Going to a new school can be difficult, especially if you join in the middle of a term. All changes take a while to get used to.

> Lauren is coming to live with us.

◀ It's Our House!

Sharing your home with a stepfamily can mean lots of changes. You may not like all of them. You may feel cross if no one asked you how you would feel about it. Try to remember that it's also strange for your new stepfamily.

> What am I going to call my new mum?

▶ What Do I Call Her?

It can be difficult knowing what to call your stepparent. He or she is not your natural parent, and you may not want to call him or her dad or mum. It is a good idea to talk about it together so that you can decide what feels right for all of you.

> I've got tickets for the match.

Story: Missing Dad

1 Keith's dad has come to pick Keith up for their weekly day out together.

> We've won!

2 Keith enjoys being with his dad, who lives with Mia, his new partner.

> What are we doing next Saturday, Dad?

> I'm sorry, son. I've got to work next weekend.

3 Keith was upset when his dad said that he could not see him next Saturday.

Why was Keith disappointed?

Keith lives with his mum and sees his dad once a week. He enjoys being with his dad. The time you spend with the parent from whom you live apart is important. It can make you feel let down, upset and angry if he or she is unable to see you. This feeling is quite natural.

► **New Babies!**

A new baby can mean lots of change, even if the baby is your natural brother or sister. But a new baby doesn't mean that your natural parent and your stepparent are going to stop loving you.

I think you've had enough sweets for one day!

But my mum never takes my sweets away.

◄ **It's All Different Now!**

You may find it difficult if your stepparent does not let you behave in the same way as your natural parent does. Try to tell both parents how you feel so you can all agree on what you are, or are not, allowed to do.

Gary, how did you cope with all the changes?

"To begin with, it was so confusing and I felt angry that everything had to change. Nothing was the same. But it was lots of change for everyone. Even though it was all scary, it was quite fun too."

Being A Family

Last week in class Julien and Brian were talking about what it means to be part of a family. They decided that in some ways being part of a stepfamily is not really that different from being part of any other family, except that you come together from two families.

All families have good days... and bad days.

▶ Sharing

In all families everybody has to learn to get along. Some people find it easier than others. In a stepfamily, just like in any other family, there will be times when you get fed up with each other.

◀ Feeling Jealous

It is quite natural for you to feel a bit jealous of a stepbrother or -sister. It may seem as if he or she is given special treatment by your parents. Try to remember that it takes time for everyone to get used to being in a stepfamily.

▶ Speak Up

Talking and listening to each other is important for all families. It can be especially important as members of a stepfamily get used to each other. Sorting out any difficulties is much easier if you talk to each other.

▶ Good Times!

It can be great fun doing things together as a family and that means a stepfamily, too! You can still enjoy being part of a stepfamily, even if you only see your stepfamily from time to time.

It's your fault.

Not it isn't. You did it!

◀ Not So Good Times!

All families have times when they get fed up with each other. But you'll feel much better about it if you don't stay cross for too long. Remember the good times and try to learn from the difficult times.

Julien, do you find it hard seeing your stepfamily only at weekends?

"It's not a problem. I love living with Dad but it's great fun going to stay with my stepfamily, as well. It can take a while before I feel really at home when I go to visit my stepfamily, but after that it's just like being in any family."

26

Story: Everyone's Happy!

1 The Brooks family were trying to organise a day out.

2 Anne decided to write down what each person wanted to do.

3 Anne's plan meant that everyone would be happy.

How did Anne manage to please everyone?

Anne's stepfamily all wanted to do something different.
She decided to make a list of what each person wanted to
do. That way, they worked out a plan which made everyone
happy. Being part of a family is much easier and more fun
if you all take time to think of each other.

Don't Forget...

1

What tips do you have about new stepparents, Charlie?

"I was really upset at my parents splitting up. I didn't want to speak to Janice, my stepmum. But when I realised that my mum and dad were not going to get back together, I started to give Janice a chance. She's like a friend now."

2

What tips do you have for getting on with stepbrothers and -sisters, Julien?

"Give them a chance because they probably feel as unsure about you as you do about them. Try not to decide straight away whether you like them or not. You may never be best of friends with them, but then again you may. You may even get on with them better than your natural brothers or sisters."

3

What do you think about all the changes you have had to make, Gary?

"I was quite angry when Dad first told me that I had to change school, move house and have a stepmum. But we had a talk and he said he was as nervous as I was about all the changes. It made it better because we both felt the same."

4

Have you got any tips for new stepfamilies, Jess?

"Try to accept the situation. It may be much better than you think. In any family, you need to work together and to talk about any problems. If you do feel uncomfortable, tell your natural parent or another grown-up who you trust."

Find Out More About Stepfamilies

Helpful Addresses and Phone Numbers

Talking about problems can really help. If you can't talk to someone close to you, then try ringing one of these organisations:

Childline
Tel: 0800 1111
A 24-hour free helpline for children. The number won't show up on a telephone bill.

National Stepfamily Association
3rd Floor, Chapel House,
18 Hatton Place, London EC1N 8RU
National Stepfamily Association provides support and information to children and adults in stepfamilies. Parents can ring its free Parentline phoneline: 0808 800 2222.

National Family Mediation
7 The Close, Exeter
Devon EX1 1EZ
NFM helps parents with their divorce as well as providing services for their children during and after separation.

Kids Helpline, Australia
Tel: 1800 55 1800
A 24-hour free helpline for children.

Stepfamily Helpline
Tel: 03 9481 1500
Australia's helpline for stepfamilies.

Stepfamily Australia
PO Box 1162, Gawler
South Australia 5118
Tel: 08 8522 7007
Advice and support for stepfamilies.

On the Web

These websites are also helpful. You can get in touch with some of them using email:

www.Itsnotyourfault.org

www.childline.org.uk

www.stepfamilies.info

www.parentlineplus.org.uk

www.nfm.org.uk

www.stepfamily.asn.au

www.stepstop.com

www.happystepfamilyday.org

www.stepfamily.org

Further Reading

Talking About: Stepfamilies by Sarah Levete (Aladdin/Watts)

How Can I Deal With: My Step Family by Sally Hewitt (Franklin Watts)

Let's Talk About It: Stepfamilies by Fred Rogers (Putnam Juvenile)

Talking It Through: My Stepfamily by Rosemary Stones (Happy Cat Books)

Boundless Grace by Mary Hoffman and Caroline Binch (Picture Puffins)

Index

Photocredits

l-left, r-right, b-bottom, t-top, c-centre, m-middle

All photos from istockphoto.com except: Cover tl & tc, 7, 15 — Digital Vision.

19, 20, 22, 28tr — DAJ. 24 , 26, 28bl— Corbis. 25 — Brand X Pictures.

All the photos in this book have been posed by models.